Built for Speed

The World's Fastest Superbikes

by Terri Sievert

Consultant:
Hugh Fleming
Director, AMA Sports
American Motorcyclist Association

CAPSTONE
HIGH-INTEREST
BOOKS

an imprint of Capstone Press
Mankato, Minnesota

Capstone High-Interest Books are published by Capstone Press
151 Good Counsel Drive, P.O. Box 669, Mankato, Minnesota 56002
http://www.capstone-press.com

Library of Congress Cataloging-in-Publication Data
Sievert, Terri.
The world's fastest superbikes/by Terri Sievert.
    p. cm.—(Built for speed)
    Includes bibliographical references and index.
    Summary: Discusses the history and development of some of the world's
fastest racing motorcycles.
    ISBN 0-7368-1060-9
    1. Motorcycles, Racing—History—Juvenile literature. [1. Motorcycles.]
I. Title. II. Built for speed (Mankato, Minn.)
TL442 .S54 2002
629.227'5—dc21   2001003245

Editorial Credits

Angela Kaelberer, editor; Karen Risch, product planning editor; Timothy Halldin,
    cover and interior designer; Katy Kudela, photo researcher

Photo Credits

American Suzuki Motor Corporation, cover, 13, 14, 16, 32, 35, 36 (top), 37 (bottom)
Courtesy of American Honda Motor Co., Inc., 26, 28, 37 (top)
Courtesy of Dave Campos, 6
Hulton/Archive Photos, 4
Kevin Wing, 10, 20, 24, 30
Michael Cooper/ALLSPORT PHOTOGRAPHY, 38
Photography supplied by Kawasaki Motors Corp., USA, 18, 23, 36 (bottom)
Robin Tuluie, 41, 42

1 2 3 4 5 6 07 06 05 04 03 02

Table of Contents

Chapter 1

Fast Motorcycles

German inventor Gottlieb Daimler built the first true motorcycle in 1885. This motorcycle had a wooden frame. The seat was a small saddle. The motorcycle had a small wheel on each side of the rear wheel. The motorcycle's seat was too high for the rider's feet to touch the ground. The small wheels kept the motorcycle from tipping.

Daimler's motorcycle was not made to go fast. It was powered by a 265cc engine. Engine size is measured in cubic centimeters (ccs). Many of today's motorcycles have engines that are 1200cc or larger.

Early Racing Motorcycles
In 1907, the world's first racetrack opened in Surrey, England. It was called Brooklands. People

Early motorcyclists raced at Brooklands.

Dave Campos holds the motorcycle speed record of 322.149 miles (518.434 kilometers) per hour.

raced both automobiles and motorcycles at this track. Companies such as Indian, Excelsior, and Harley-Davidson made many of the first racing motorcycles.

In the 1960s, many racers began to use motorcycles made in Japan. Japanese companies make most of today's top racing motorcycles. These companies include Honda, Suzuki, Yamaha, and Kawasaki.

Speed Record

On July 14, 1990, Dave Campos set the motorcycle speed record. He reached a speed of 322.149 miles (518.434 kilometers) per hour.

Campos set the record with a streamliner motorcycle. It was shaped like a torpedo. Campos sat inside an enclosed area called a cockpit. The motorcycle was 23 feet (7 meters) long. It weighed 2,500 pounds (1,135 kilograms). It had two Ruxton Harley-Davidson 1500cc engines.

Campos' motorcycle was not practical for driving on streets or highways. But some fast motorcycles are designed to ride both on racetracks and roads. These motorcycles are called superbikes.

Superbikes are production motorcycles. Motorcycle companies produce large numbers of them to sell to the public. Most superbike racers make changes to their production motorcycles to make them travel faster.

The fastest superbikes are the Suzuki GSX1300R, the Kawasaki ZX-12R, the Honda CBR1100XX, and the Suzuki GSX-R1000. The GSX1300R is the fastest of these powerful motorcycles.

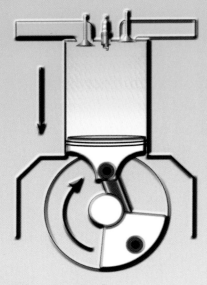

1. Intake

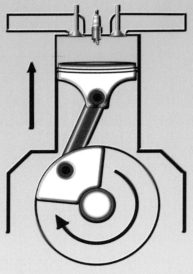

2. Compression

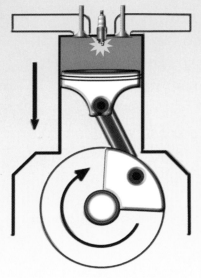

3. Combustion

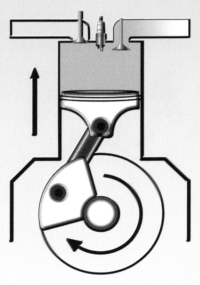

4. Exhaust

Motorcycle engines can have from one to four cylinders. These hollow chambers are shaped like cans. They hold devices called pistons. Engines with more cylinders usually produce more power.

Motorcycles can have two-stroke or four-stroke engines. Some smaller motorcycles such as dirt bikes have two-stroke engines. Superbikes have four-stroke engines. Fuel ignites on every second stroke in a two-stroke engine. It ignites on every fourth stroke in a four-stroke engine.

Fuel must mix with air before it will burn. Each movement of the piston within the cylinder is called a stroke. The piston first moves down. This action opens the intake valve and allows air and fuel to enter the cylinder. The piston then moves up and pushes together the fuel and air. This action is called compression. A spark from the spark plugs then ignites this mixture. This action is called combustion. The piston then moves down and allows the burned gases to escape. These gases are called exhaust.

The fuel creates power as it burns. The power turns the wheels and makes the motorcycle move forward.

The rider controls the speed of the motorcycle with the throttle. The throttle sends fuel to the engine.

9

Chapter 2

Suzuki GSX1300R

The Suzuki GSX1300R Hayabusa is named after a type of Japanese falcon. This bird can dive at almost 200 miles (322 kilometers) per hour. The motorcycle's top speed is nearly that fast.

The Hayabusa is powerful. The motorcycle can reach 60 miles (97 kilometers) per hour in 2.6 seconds. Its top speed is 194 miles (312 kilometers) per hour. Its design allows riders to handle the bike well even at these high speeds.

Suzuki began making the Hayabusa in 1999. The motorcycle earned several awards for its performance. These awards included *Motorcyclist* magazine's 1999 Motorcycle of

The Hayabusa is the world's fastest superbike.

the Year and *Cycle World* magazine's 1999
Best Superbike.

Design

The Hayabusa's frame is made of a lightweight
metal called aluminum. The frame also is
called the chassis. The Hayabusa has a
twin-spar frame. Two large pieces of aluminum
wrap around and support the engine. These
hollow spars are both lightweight and strong.

A fairing covers the Hayabusa's sides and
front. This smooth shield is made of a sturdy
material called ABS plastic. The fairing makes
the motorcycle aerodynamic. It helps the
motorcycle cut through the air.

The Hayabusa has a vertical headlight.
The large, narrow headlight is shaped like
a diamond.

Engine

A liquid-cooled 1299cc engine powers the
Hayabusa. This engine has four cylinders.
It uses a mixture of oil and air to cool
the engine. The engine can produce

The Hayabusa's fairing helps the motorcycle cut through the air.

160 horsepower. This unit measures an engine's power. Most production motorcycles produce about 120 to 130 horsepower.

In the past, most automobiles and motorcycles had a carburetor. This device mixes the proper amounts of gasoline and air needed to power the engine. Today, many automobiles and motorcycles have a fuel injection system instead of a carburetor. Fuel injection systems use

The Hayabusa's ram air intake is close to the center of the fairing.

devices called throttle bodies. Throttle bodies have valves that spray fuel directly into the engine's cylinders. The Hayabusa's fuel injection system has four throttle bodies. One fuel injector sprays each cylinder.

The Hayabusa has an electronic fuel injection system. Electronic sensors gather information about the engine speed and outside air temperature and pressure. These sensors help the throttle bodies spray the right amount of fuel into the cylinders.

Ram Air Intake

Air mixes with fuel through a ram air system. Air enters the engine through openings in the bike. These openings are called the ram air intake. Most superbikes have this feature. But some motorcycles have the air intake at the rear of the bike. The bike's exhaust system warms the air at the rear of the bike. A rear air intake may let this hot air into the engine.

The Hayabusa's ram air intake is located on the front of the bike. This intake lets cool air into the engine. This cool air helps increase the motorcycle's horsepower. The Hayabusa's ram air intake is close to the center of the fairing. Air pressure is highest in this area when the bike is in motion. The air enters a plastic airbox located beneath the gas tank before it goes into the engine.

The Hayabusa has an adjustable suspension system.

Suspension System

A motorcycle's suspension system supports the bike's chassis. This system also helps absorb bumps to make the ride comfortable.

The front of the chassis rests on shock absorbers called forks. These metal tubes keep the bike stable and help it turn corners. The forks are telescopic. The smaller part of the fork slides into the larger part. Springs inside the fork legs absorb bumps. The forks also are inverted. The thicker part is on top. The thinner part is on the bottom. This feature helps make the motorcycle stable. The Hayabusa also has a shock absorber on the rear wheel. It contains a spring surrounded by oil.

The Hayabusa's suspension system is adjustable. Riders can adjust the forks and the shock springs to make the ride smoother or rougher. A bike with a rough ride often can reach higher speeds than one with a smooth ride.

Brakes

The Hayabusa has disc brakes on both the front and back wheels. The discs are round pieces of steel attached to the wheels. Clamps called calipers also connect to the wheels. The brake pads are on the calipers. Pistons push the calipers into the discs when the rider presses the brake. The brake pads grip the discs. This action creates friction. The friction slows down the motorcycle.

The Hayabusa has a large front brake. Brake size is measured in millimeters. The front brake has two 320-millimeter discs. Each disc attaches to a six-piston caliper. The back brake has one 240-millimeter disc. This disc's caliper has two pistons.

Chapter 3

Kawasaki ZX-12R

Kawasaki produced the first ZX-12R Ninja in 1999. The Ninja's top speed is 190 miles (306 kilometers) per hour. It can reach 60 miles (97 kilometers) per hour in 2.7 seconds.

Kawasaki engineers designed the Ninja to reduce air resistance. The engineers tested the motorcycle in a wind tunnel.

In a wind tunnel, a large fan blows air past the motorcycle. The engineers add smoke to this air. The smoke allows the engineers to see how the air moves around the motorcycle. They then can change the motorcycle's design to make it more aerodynamic.

The Ninja's top speed is 190 miles (306 kilometers) per hour.

The Ninja's fairing has an aerodynamic design.

Design

The Ninja has an aluminum frame that is lightweight and narrow. It also is stiff and strong. The motorcycle's narrow design makes it aerodynamic.

The ZX-12R's fairing also has an aerodynamic design. Small wings extend from the sides of the fairing. The wings help the air sweep past the bike.

Frame

The Ninja ZX-12R has a monocoque chassis. This frame is different from most motorcycles. Most motorcycles have a twin-spar frame.

The Ninja's frame is shaped like a rectangle. It has four aluminum plates that are welded together. The frame wraps around the outside of the engine. The airbox, air filter, and battery box are all inside the frame. These parts take up less space when placed inside the frame.

The monocoque chassis makes the Ninja narrower than other superbikes. Its narrow body makes it more aerodynamic.

Engine

The Ninja ZX-12R has a liquid-cooled 1199cc engine. The engine can produce more than 180 horsepower.

Electronic sensors make the throttle respond quickly to the rider's commands. The sensors detect the air pressure outside the motorcycle.

Sensors also detect the throttle position and the engine's speed and temperature. The sensors send information to a control system. This system controls the throttle bodies' mixture of fuel and air.

The Ninja's ram air intake is under the headlight. The airbox is in front of the rider. This location is different from most motorcycles. The Ninja's airbox is placed where the gas tank sits on many motorcycles. The Ninja's gas tank is under the seat. This position lowers the Ninja's center of gravity. A lower center of gravity improves the bike's turning and handling.

Suspension System and Brakes

The Ninja's front suspension system has inverted telescopic adjustable forks. These forks are made of aluminum.

The Ninja's rear wheel has single-shock suspension. The shock absorber contains one spring surrounded by oil. This wheel also has

The Ninja's extra-wide rear tire improves the bike's traction.

an extra-wide tire for better traction. The wide tire grips the road better than narrower tires.

The Ninja's front brake has two 320-millimeter discs with six-piston calipers. The rear brake has one 230-millimeter disc and a caliper with two pistons.

Chapter 4

Honda
CBR1100XX

The Honda CBR1100XX also is called the Double X in the United States. In Europe and Canada, it is called the Super Blackbird. This name comes from the Lockheed SR-71 Blackbird spy plane. The plane's top speed was about 2,190 miles per hour (3,500 kilometers per hour).

Honda introduced the Double X in 1997. Its top speed is 177 miles (285 kilometers) per hour. This speed is not as fast as the top speed of newer high performance motorcycles.

Honda has produced the Double X since 1997.

The Double X is available in red.

The Double X may not beat newer bikes on a drag strip. Riders test their motorcycles' speeds on these long, straight paved tracks. But it easily keeps up with them during normal traveling conditions. According to magazine tests, the Double X can reach 60 miles (97 kilometers) per hour in 2.6 seconds.

Design

The Double X is shaped like a bullet with wings on its tail end. This shape lets it slice through the air.

The Double X has other design features that improve its aerodynamics. Its short windshield is tilted back to allow air to flow around it. The motorcycle's handlebars angle down to allow the rider to lean close to the bike. The footpegs are high and set toward the back of the bike. This position shelters the rider's feet from the wind. It also keeps the rider's feet out of the way when the bike turns a corner.

The Double X has one tall, narrow headlight. The headlight's position allows the bike to have a narrow, aerodynamic front end.

The Double X has an aluminum twin-spar diamond frame. The engine is not supported by metal spars. This design makes the motorcycle lightweight. The engine also is easier to repair without the additional spars.

Honda has produced the Double X in many colors in North America and Europe. These colors include black, silver, and red.

The Double X's engine produces 133 horsepower.

Engine

The CBR1100XX has an 1137cc engine. The liquid-cooled engine has four cylinders and an electronic fuel injection system. The engine produces 133 horsepower.

The Double X has a ram air system. Its two large air ducts send air to the airbox and the electronic fuel injection system.

Suspension and Brakes

The Double X's front frame suspension is a 43-millimeter telescopic fork. It has a single adjustable rear shock absorber.

The Double X has two 310-millimeter front disc brakes with three-piston calipers. The rear brake is a 256-millimeter single disc brake with a three-piston caliper.

On most motorcycles, the front and rear brakes work separately. But the Double X's front and rear brakes are linked. Both brakes come on when a rider either squeezes the front brake lever on the handlebar or presses the rear foot pedal. This combined action can improve the brakes' performance in an emergency.

Chapter 5

Suzuki GSX-R1000

Before 2001, Suzuki produced the GSX-R750 and the larger GSX-R1100. The GSX-R750 handled well on the racetrack. The GSX-R1100's powerful engine allowed the bike to reach high speeds.

Some riders wanted the powerful GSX-R1100 engine in a smaller frame. These riders put a GSX-R1100 engine into a GSX-R750 frame. They called this motorcycle a "7-11."

In 2001, Suzuki decided to make a bike that was like the 7-11. The company replaced the GSX-R1100 with the GSX-R1000. This bike looks much like the GSX-R750. The two motorcycles are nearly the same size. Their engines are similar. But the R1000's 988cc engine provides more power than the R750's 749cc engine.

The GSX-R1000's short wheelbase makes it ideal for performing wheelies.

The GSX-R1000 is shorter and narrower than many superbikes.

Design

The GSX-R1000 can reach a speed of 176 miles (283 kilometers) per hour. The engine produces about 150 horsepower.

The GSX-R1000 is shorter and narrower than many superbikes. The bike is 80.5 inches (204 centimeters) long and 28.1 inches (71 centimeters) wide.

The GSX-R1000 has a shorter wheelbase than many superbikes. Its wheelbase measures 55.5 inches (141 centimeters). The bike's short wheelbase makes it ideal for doing wheelies. During a wheelie, a rider lifts the front tire off the ground. Professional riders can do wheelies on the bike at about 140 miles (225 kilometers) per hour.

The GSX-R1000 is lighter than many other superbikes. It weighs 375 pounds (170 kilograms). This weight is about 100 pounds (45 kilograms) less than the Hayabusa's weight.

The GSX-R1000 has a lightweight aluminum twin-spar frame. The front of the GSX-R1000 is narrow. The rear is small and lightweight. This design makes the motorcycle aerodynamic.

Suzuki produces the GSX-R1000 in several colors. In North America, the bike is available in blue and white. It also is available in black and silver. Suzuki makes a red and silver model sold only in Europe.

Engine

The GSX-R1000 uses a 988cc liquid-cooled engine. The engine in the GSX-R1000 is similar to the engine in the GSX-R750. But it is slightly larger and heavier.

The motorcycle has ram air intake ducts. Air enters the engine through intake snorkels. These devices are near the center of the fairing. Air pressure is the highest in this area.

Most fuel injection systems have one butterfly valve. The rider turns the throttle to open the butterfly valve. This action increases the bike's speed.

The GSX-R1000 has two butterfly valves inside each of its four throttle bodies. The throttle controls one valve in each throttle body. An onboard computer controls the other valve. The computer receives information from the engine. It checks the gear and the engine speed. It opens the second valve when the rider opens the throttle. This action keeps the fuel and air mixture at the right level.

Suspension System and Brakes

The GSX-R1000's front frame rests on adjustable inverted forks. The fork tubes are coated in a lightweight metal called titanium-nitride. The coating reduces friction

The GSX-R1000's fork tubes are coated in a metal called titanium-nitride.

between the fork tube and the oil seal. This feature makes the bike react better to small bumps in the road.

The GSX-R1000 has two 320-millimeter disc brakes on the front wheel. The calipers are similar to those on the Hayabusa. But the calipers on the GSX-R1000 are lighter than those of the Hayabusa. The rear brake has a 220-millimeter disc with a two-piston caliper.

FAST FACTS

SUZUKI GSX1300R HAYABUSA

Engine Size:	1299cc
Horsepower:	160
Length:	84.3 inches (214 centimeters)
Width:	29.1 inches (74 centimeters)
Weight:	474 pounds (215 kilograms)
Top Speed:	194 miles (312 kilometers) per hour

KAWASAKI ZX-12R NINJA

Engine Size:	1199cc
Horsepower:	180
Length:	81.9 inches (208 centimeters)
Width:	28.5 inches (72 centimeters)
Weight:	463 pounds (210 kilograms)
Top Speed:	190 miles (306 kilometers) per hour

HONDA CBR1100XX

Engine Size: 1137cc

Horsepower: 133

Length: 85 inches
(216 centimeters)

Width: 28.3 inches
(72 centimeters)

Weight: 492 pounds
(223 kilograms)

Top Speed: 177 miles (285
kilometers) per hour

SUZUKI GSX-R1000

Engine Size: 988cc

Horsepower: 150

Length: 80.5 inches
(204 centimeters)

Width: 28.1 inches
(71 centimeters)

Weight: 375 pounds
(170 kilograms)

Top Speed: 176 miles (283
kilometers) per hour

Chapter 6

Future of Fast Superbikes

Today's motorcycles are fast. But motorcycle companies believe that they can build faster motorcycles. These motorcycles may have bigger engines and more aerodynamic frames than today's motorcycles.

Some people do not believe that companies should build faster motorcycles. Riders sometimes drive faster than the speed limit. High-speed crashes often are deadly.

Higher Speeds
Most motorcycles cannot travel faster than 200 miles (322 kilometers) per hour. But some

Most motorcycles cannot travel faster than 200 miles (322 kilometers) per hour.

companies are developing motorcycles that can reach that speed or faster.

In the future, small companies may produce the fastest motorcycles. Large companies face pressure from the government and safety organizations to limit their bikes' speeds. Small companies have more freedom to produce a small number of fast motorcycles.

Tul-aris

In 1997, Dr. Robin Tuluie began work on a new type of motorcycle. At the time, Tuluie was an engineer at Polaris, Inc., in Roseau, Minnesota. This company makes recreational vehicles such as four-wheelers, jet skis, and snowmobiles.

Tuluie and a team of friends designed and built a new racing motorcycle. They used parts of a Polaris snowmobile engine. Tuluie's team finished work on the motorcycle in 2000. Tuluie called the new bike the Tul-aris. The motorcycle's name is a combination of his last name and Polaris.

In 1997, Dr. Robin Tuluie began work on a new type of motorcycle.

Tuluie has entered the Tul-aris in several motorcycle races.

The Tul-aris is faster than many production superbikes. Its top speed is 190 miles (306 kilometers) per hour. The 780cc engine produces 173 horsepower.

The Tul-aris is long and narrow. It is 79.9 inches (203 centimeters) long and only 22 inches (56 centimeters) wide. The bike's design makes it aerodynamic.

In March 2000, professional rider Michael Barnes raced the Tul-aris at Daytona International Speedway in Daytona, Florida. Tuluie also has entered the bike in several other motorcycle races. But he currently does not plan to produce the Tul-aris for sale to the public.

Y2K

A Louisiana company called Marine Turbine Technologies makes a motorcycle that can reach very high speeds. The Y2K Turbine superbike has a top speed of 266 miles (428 kilometers) per hour.

The Y2K has a Rolls-Royce Allison turbine gas engine. Some helicopters also use this engine. It produces more than 320 horsepower.

The Y2K is much heavier and longer than standard superbikes. It weighs 460 pounds (209 kilograms). Its wheelbase is nearly 71 inches (180 centimeters) long.

People can buy the Y2K from motorcycle dealers. But it is much more expensive than standard superbikes. Most superbikes cost between $10,000 and $12,000. The Y2K's price is $150,000.

Words to Know

aerodynamic (air-oh-dye-NAM-mik)—designed to move quickly and easily through the air

calipers (KAL-uh-purss)—a set of clamps at the end of a brake cable; calipers press against a wheel to stop it from turning.

chassis (CHASS-ee)—the frame on which the body of a vehicle is built

cylinder (SIL-uhn-dur)—a hollow chamber in an engine in which fuel burns to create power

piston (PIS-tuhn)—a part inside an engine cylinder that moves up and down as fuel burns

sensor (SEN-sur)—an electronic device that detects information such as air pressure and sends it to the motorcycle's control system

throttle (THROT-uhl)—a valve in a vehicle's engine that opens to let steam, fuel, or fuel and air flow into the engine; the throttle controls the vehicle's speed.

To Learn More

Hendrickson, Steve. *Land Speed Racing.*
Motorcycles. Mankato, Minn.: Capstone
High-Interest Books, 2000.

Oxlade, Chris. *Cars, Trains, and Motorcycles.*
How Science Works. Brookfield, Conn.:
Copper Beech Books, 2000.

Pupeza, Lori Kinstad. *Sport Bikes.*
Ultimate Motorcycle. Edina, Minn.:
Abdo & Daughters, 1999.

Youngblood, Ed. *Superbike Racing.*
Motorcycles. Mankato, Minn.: Capstone
High-Interest Books, 2000.

Useful Addresses

American Motorcyclist Association
13515 Yarmouth Drive
Pickerington, OH 43147

Canadian Motorcycle Association
P.O. Box 448
Hamilton, ON L8L 1J4
Canada

**National Motorcycle Museum and Hall
  of Fame**
200 East Main Street
P.O. Box 405
Anamosa, IA 52205

Internet Sites

American Motorcyclist Association
http://www.ama-cycle.org

Canadian Motorcycle Association
http://www.canmocycle.ca

Motorcycle Daily
http://www.motorcycledaily.com

National Motorcycle Museum and Hall of Fame
http://www.nationalmcmuseum.org

Index